Secrets an̲d̲ ̲T̲r̲e̲a̲s̲u̲r̲e̲s̲

Northam̲

A county guide
to the unusual

by
Mia Butler

S.B. Publications

By the same author
Northamptonshire Rambles
Let's Go Walkabout in Northamptonshire
Exploring the Nene Way

To my friend and advisor, Colin Eaton, who would not, and could not, be fazed

First published in 1996 by S. B. Publications
c/o 19 Grove Road, Seaford, East Sussex BN25 1TP

ISBN 1 85770 106 2

Typeset by CGB, Lewes

Printed and bound by MFP Design & Print
Longford Trading Estate, Thomas Street,
Stretford, Manchester M32 0JT.
Tel: 0161 864 4540

CONTENTS

NORTHAMPTON

OUNDLE

WELLINGBOROUGH

ACKNOWLEDGEMENTS
Photographs by Colin Eaton and David Rhodes, Marian Pipe,
Irchester Narrow Gauge Railway Trust, John Russell, Joyce Palmer.

BIBLIOGRAPHY
Royal Commission on Historical Monuments *Archaeological Sites of
Northamptonshire. Volumes I-IV.*
The Northamptonshire Village Book. Northamptonshire Federation of
Womens' Institutes.
The Buildings of England – Northamptonshire by Nikolaus Pevsner.

*Front cover: One of a pair of white swans made of cast iron that are on the gate pillars
at the drive entrance to Lamport Hall. (See page 50)*

Title page: Unusual traffic sign in Denford High Street.

Back cover: Flying Fortress memorial window in the church at Grafton Underwood.

INTRODUCTION

MY initial thoughts at the outset of this project was: Where to begin? However, it proved to be no problem to dream up a long list of items of interest – it was rather harder to decide which to leave out.

Owing to my own innately inquisitive nature, this offering has been a pleasure to produce and satisfied a long-filled ambition to share the accumulation of my personal knowledge, and that of willing others, of the bizarre and unexpected in my home county.

Northamptonshire is a storehouse of infinite scope and diversity and should be enjoyed for the delights it offers. Most simply require little more than an inquiring mind and a desire to adventure into this intriguing shire of squires and spires. Some reflect genteel echoes of a bygone age and some are more modern and some faintly brash.

The 'treasures' recorded on these pages are there for all to see. They are grouped by district, as indicated in the table of contents, to make it easy to plan sightseeing visits in a given area. Suggested access points and Ordnance Survey map references (Landranger series 1 50 000) and approximate mileages are also given.

Since the idea of this book was first mooted, one of the items that was to be featured, the Arms of the Leather Trade, has disappeared. The building on which it was mounted was demolished and it was presumably destroyed. Other items mentioned may have subsequently suffered vandalism or defacement – one can make no guarantees.

DEENETHORPE – USAAF WARTIME AIRFIELD MEMORIAL

> *Location*: On the A427 east of Corby, between Weldon and Benefield.
> OS 141 953897

VAST tracts of farmland were hastily converted to airfields in the grim years of World War II and immense runways of concrete were laid over fields where previously cattle had grazed and for centuries crops had ripened undisturbed. Soon the drone of gigantic B17 bombers, coming and going on their vital sorties, became commonplace.

The granite memorial to Station 126 – Deenethorpe, was dedicated in 1989. It stands at the edge of the airfield from which the 401st Bombardment Group flew 254 combat missions over Germany and Occupied Europe between October 1943 to May 1945.

The group was awarded two Distinguished Unit Citations and the inscription on the memorial records it as: 'THE BEST DAMNED OUTFIT IN THE USAAF'. A network of eight airfields straddled the county, scarring the picturesque scenery, but now, fifty years on, much of the land has been returned to agricultural use.

Nostalgia continues to bring back from the New World some of those who served in England in wartime – to pay tribute to their comrades and recall fraught, but perhaps precious days, in a foreign land.

EAST CARLTON COUNTRY PARK – STEEL INGOTS

Location: Off the A427 four and a half miles west of Corby, on the Market Harborough Road. OS 141 832896

THESE massive steel ingots form only a small part of the display of early industrial equipment on the cobbled forecourt outside the craft workshop in East Carlton Country Park, which is open all the year round.

Other items include a gigantic bucket, said to be able to hold an entire football team, from one of the famous 'walking draglines' excavators with which quarries were once equipped.

In the Heritage Centre there are both static and working models of the famous Corby steelworks. The craft workshop, which was opened in 1983 by Corby District Council, is staffed by craft workers skilled in the various trades and on the ground floor the resident blacksmith can be seen at work.

East Carlton Hall was built on the lines of a French chateau in 1870 on the site of a late Palladian period house. It was designed by architect Edmund Francis Law, a one time mayor of Northampton, and became the seat of the Palmer family, who turned successfully from farming to the manufacture of biscuits. It is now a private house.

MIDDLETON HILL – HORSE TROUGH

Location: Three and a half miles west of Corby, off the A427 Corby to Market Harborough Road. OS 141 840897

THIS handsome drinking trough, nestling in the long stone wall, its spring still trickling away, must have been a welcome stop for horses labouring up the steep hill. On it is the inscription:

IHP
1844.

The initials are presumably those of the donor, a member of the Palmer family who used to live at East Carlton Hall.

STANION – THE PONDEROUS RIB

Location: Outside St Peter's Church. East of the A43 Corby to Kettering road.
OS 141 915868

IN the guardianship of this late thirteenth church, with its slender broach spire, lies what is said to be a cow's rib. This enormous bone, of great weight and taller than a man, seems more suited to the whale or even an elephant.

The story goes that the good-natured dun cow to which it belonged gave unlimited supplies of milk to nourish the poor people of the parish over many years. The local witch – in those days every rural community had one – challenged this claim and said that she would prove that the animal would not be able to fill her pail.

She craftily placed a vessel with holes in its base beneath the patient cow. It acted like a sieve and as fast as the cow produced milk it drained away. The animal died of exhaustion and was sadly missed by the villagers.

One of the quarries in the vicinity is said to be known locally as Cowthick Quarry – perhaps as a lingering memorial to the kindly cow.

WELDON – LOCK-UP AND LANTERN TOWER

Location: Two miles east of Corby on the A427 to Oundle. OS 141 928894

THE lock-up or roundhouse, pictured left, was used in the eighteenth and early nineteenth century as a place of detention for miscreants.

Its sturdy, cylindrical walls are made of Weldon stone and the conical roof would surely thwart any attempts of escape from within or rescue from without.

Offenders were incarcerated overnight after arrest by an elected constable, and either brought before the magistrate the next day or simply left to reflect upon their misdeeds.

THE village of Weldon-in-the-Woods stood in the heart of the vast Rockingham Forest.

The church of St Mary the Virgin, right, dates from the thirteenth century and it is crowned with a domed lantern tower, the light from which acted as a beacon for travellers making their way through the forest.

Nearby, across Willow Brook, is Haunt Hill House. It is built of the limestone which has been quarried here since the Middle Ages, and has a mason's date stone of the year 1643.

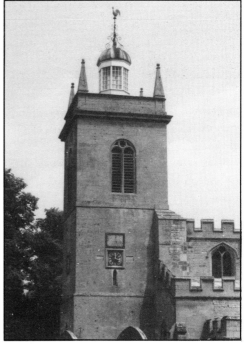

WILBARSTON – DOVECOTE

Location: Fork right off the A427 west from Corby on to the B669 to Stoke Albany
OS 141 812884

ON the far side of the primary school grounds is this group of seven rows of open pigeon-holes set in the boundary wall – all that remains of a post-medieval rectangular dovecote or columbarium.

These structures would, on average, house 500 pairs of birds. They were built close to the manor house, as part of the regular farm buildings, for in the days when hay was unknown and cattle slaughtered in the autumn, pigeons provided fresh meat for the household in winter.

The dovecote is a County Heritage Site to which the public has access. Visitors should obtain permission to view from the school office during term time, otherwise entry may be gained through metal gates from a side lane around the corner.

AYNHO – CARTWRIGHT GRAVE

Location: St Michael's Church, Aynho, the southernmost village in the county on the A 41 south east of Banbury. OS 151 515331

THE Cartwrights were lords of the manor of Aynho for 300 years and there are a number of monuments to them in the church, which was rebuilt in 1725 by Edward Wing, a disciple of Sir Christopher Wren.

This highly ornate wrought iron grave marker is in the churchyard and on the shield on the central column, beneath a coronet, denoting the rank of the occupant of the grave, is the inscription:

**Here lies the body of
Marie Elizabeth
Auguste Cartwright
Eldest daughter of
Captain Count
Sandizell
of Sandizell, Bavaria
And widow of the late
Sir Thomas Cartwright
GCH
Born Feb 20th 1805
Died April 13th 1902**

RIP

BADBY – ARCH

Location: East of the village, off the minor road to Everdon. OS 152 563588

THIS stone arch stands in splendid isolation at the entrance to Badby Wood. When originally constructed early in the nineteenth century there were rooms on either side of the entrance. The gatekeeper and his wife had their living quarters on one side of the arch and their sleeping accommodation on the opposite side.

There used to be a doorway on each inner side of the edifice so the occupants could cross from one side to the other under the shelter of the arch. The last tenants left in 1890 and the rooms were demolished about 1940.

Badby Woods are noted for their bluebells and wood anemones in early summer and for the blossom on the avenue of cherry trees planted by Lady Knightley of Fawsley Hall.

BADBY – LANTERN HOUSE

Location: Beside the A361 Daventry to Banbury road, about half a mile south of Badby. OS 152 554585

THE quaint octagonal Lantern House at the entrance to Badby Wood and plantation used to be one of the lodges of the estate owned by the Knightley family of Fawsley for many generations.

It was built around 1822 and after the death of the last tenant in 1956 it was abandoned and left to crumble. In 1980 it was completely rebuilt and is now a private house.

Nearby: On the 735ft high Arbury Hill, half a mile to the north west, is one of the county's greatest earthworks – a twenty four acre Iron Age hill fort surrounded by ramparts and a wide ditch.

BRAUNSTON – CROSS-LEGGED KNIGHT

Location: All Saints Church is on the hill beside the A45 Daventry to Coventry road. OS 152 536661

ALL SAINTS Church, a massive edifice crowning the hill and affording a panoramic view over the neighbouring county of Warwickshire, was rebuilt for the third time in 1849.

There is an unusual variety of coloured marble and alabaster in the pulpit and font and the chancel arcade is built of medieval masonry.

In the south chapel, beyond the arcade, is a relic from an earlier church. Under a canopy is a curious effigy in stone of a knight in chain mail, with sword and shield, and 'much cross-legged'.

Crusader knights were generally portrayed on their tombs in a reclining posture with legs crossed. William de Ros, who succumbed while travelling to the Holy Land in 1352, has his legs crossed in a most contorted and uncomfortable fashion.

Also from an earlier church is a massive parish chest with three heavy locks.

Nearby is the Grand Union Canal and Museum and interesting twin iron bridges on the towpath to the east.

CHARWELTON – PACKHORSE BRIDGE

THE first bridge to carry travellers between Banbury and Daventry across the River Cherwell, which rises here – in the cellar of Cherwell House – was built more than 700 years ago. It stills survives beside the modern road but is limited to pedestrian use only.

This splendid example of a medieval packhorse bridge, of which there are at least ten in the county, is one wagon width wide and built on solid masonry. The twin sharply-pointed and chamfered arches with a single cut-water between them are typical of the work of masons of the fourteenth century.

Nearby is Everdon Hall, home of the annual Everdon Horse Trials.

CULWORTH – RINGWORK OF A NORMAN CASTLE

Location: For Culworth turn right turn off the B4525 from Northampton to Banbury, about three and a half miles after Morton Pinkney. OS 152 546470

BETWEEN the 600 year old St Mary's Church and the school founded in the 1840s by Meriel d'Anvers, is a footpath which leads to this moated mound – all that now remains of a castle built by a Norman noble in post Conquest days.

On the grass verge by the wall of the Manor House lies Charlie's Pebble, the stone said to have been used by King Charles I to review his troops and to mount his horse before riding off to the Battle of Cropredy Bridge in June 1644.

The king had arrived in the village at the head of 10,000 men and spent four nights as the guest of the lord of the manor, Sir Samuel d'Anvers, a keen supporter of the Royalist cause.

EYDON – STOCKS AND WHIPPING POST

Location: Turn due west off the A4525 Northampton to Banbury road at Canons Ashby. OS 152 542500

THE old stocks and whipping post on the village green, now a County Heritage Site, date from the days when public vilification and humiliation was considered a fitting punishment for the perpetrators of quite minor crimes.

By the fifteenth century there were stocks in every town and village. They were used to hold offenders until they were brought to trial as well as to expose rogues and vagabonds to whatever their fellow human beings wanted to throw at them.

Nearby Eydon Hall, designed by James Lewis, was built for the Reverend Francis Annesley around 1790.

FAWSLEY – HA-HA

Location: St Mary's church, Fawsley, a turning off the A361 Daventry to Banbury Road about one mile south of Badby. OS 152 566568

MAROONED on a grassy knoll and surrounded by a ha-ha or submerged fence, is the church of St Mary. The hamlet it served has long since vanished.

The ha-ha, not too rare in this county, takes its name from *haya* – the Old English word for hedge. It consists of a wall of stone, with the top at ground level and the base in the ditch, serving as a barrier to animals who might invade the mound.

There are many treasures in the church, including a bible carved in stone and six heraldic shields in stained glass showing the Washington arms quartered with those of the families into which they married. The arms were brought here from Sulgrave Manor and in their blazoning are the Stars and Stripes.

Fawsley Hall, across the parkland, is the former seat of the powerful Knightley family, who lived here from 1416 to 1938. Sir Richard Knightley, as Deputy Lord Lieutenant of the county, was in attendance at the burial of Mary, Queen of Scots, at Peterborough Cathedral in 1587.

FLORE – WATTLE AND DAUB WALL

Location: Turn downhill into the village from the A45 Northampton to Daventry road. OS 152 647600

THE A45, once a turnpike, now bisects the village and on the curve of the lane, just below the scout hall, a short length of the Nene Way is flanked by a wall of wattle and daub.

Such walls are traditionally thatched to protect the material of which they are built, which may be reed, straw, rods or twigs bound together with mud or clay. They have to be carefully maintained in order to survive the elements.

The Way leads on to Nether Heyford through a the little iron kissing-gate opening on to meadowland.

NETHER HEYFORD – MORGAN MEMORIAL

Location: Church of St Peter and St Paul, Nether Heyford, south off the A45
Northampton to Daventry road. OS 152 659588

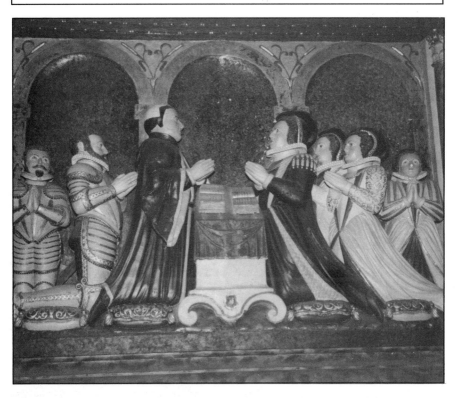

ON the wall of the south aisle of the church is this magnificent Tudor monument, in brightly painted alabaster, to the memory of Sir Francis Morgan, who was made a judge in 1556. He is depicted, in scarlet robes and wearing his judicial wig, kneeling at a prayer desk, facing his wife. Behind him are his two sons, behind her their three daughters.

It has been claimed that Sir Francis was the judge who pronounced the sentence of death on Lady Jane Grey in 1553. However, it was, in fact, Sir Richard Morgan, Lord Chief Justice of the Common Pleas, who passed sentence and, burdened with remorse, died by his own hand in 1554.

NEWNHAM – BELL PORCH

Location: St Michael and All Angels in the High Street. Newnham is on the B4037, about one mile south of Daventry . OS 152 581598

THE arches of the fifteenth century battlemented open bell tower form the entrance porch to the church of St Michael and All Angels.
It was here the bellringers stood to pull on the ropes which passed through holes in the floor above to the bells at the top of the tower.
The Nene Way, a seventy mile walk through the county, begins (or ends) in the neighbouring village of Badby.
It passes along the main street of Newnham and its passage is marked by a disc on a post at the church gate.
The Way wends through the Nene Valley, hence its name, to the northern county boundary at Wansford, from where it continues into Cambridgeshire and ultimately to The Wash.

WHILTON – CLOCK

Location: Church of St Mary, Whilton, which is just off Nobottle Belt, the old Roman road, from Northampton to Daventry. OS 152 637648

A STRIKING timepiece indeed: So what might the problem be? This spectacular blue-faced clock only displays four minutes between each of the twelve numerals – making for a very shortened hour.

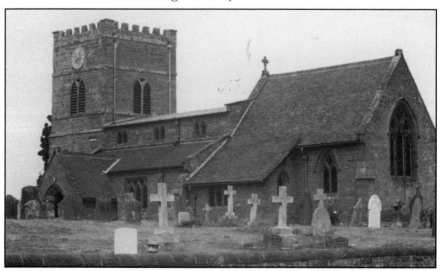

WEEDON LOIS – SITWELL HEADSTONE

Location: St Marys churchyard. Weedon Lois is on minor road from Coalworth and east of Towcester. OS 152 601470

ON the perimeter of the extended cemetery of St Mary's Church, over-looking the medieval fishponds, is the grave of poet and prose writer Dame Edith Sitwell, who died in 1964.

Her brother Sacheverell, to whom she was devoted, lived with his wife, Georgia, at nearby Weston Hall, and she stayed with them there many times.

Dominating the grave is the tall headstone on which is mounted a bronze plaque of two hands, a woman's and a child's, representing youth and age. It is the work of the celebrated sculptor, Henry Moore.

Into the stone beneath are carved the last lines of Edith Sitwell's poem *The Wind of Early Spring*

The past and present
are as one –
Accordant and discordant,
Youth and age,
And death and birth.
For out of one comes all –
From all comes one.

BRAYBROOKE – WOODEN EFFIGY OF A KNIGHT

Location: In All Saints' Church at Braybrooke, three miles south east of Market Harborough. OS 141 766845

JUST above the bridge is the church of All Saints' which is a veritable treasure house of pieces from the past. Foremost among them is a wonderfully preserved wooden effigy of a fourteenth century Crusader, Sir Thomas le Latymer.

It is one of very few wooden figures still in existence in this country and has been carved from single log of oak. In the barred alcove behind his tomb is a huge funeral helmet, the headpiece made from a single sheet of iron.

There are some traces of a wall painting on the walls of the south aisle and fragments of medieval glasss and some important documents were kept in a chest bound with iron.

An Elizabethan monument erected in memory of Sir Thomas Griffin, died 1566, and his father Sir Nicholas, died 1509, who succeeded the Latymers at Braybrooke Castle, portrays the family coat of arms and heraldic griffins.

BRAYBROOKE – RIVER JORDAN BRIDGE

STRANGE though it may seem the River Jordan flows through the heart of Braybrooke.

Within a bowshot of one side of its narrow channel faint earthworks identify the site of Braybrooke Castle, originally the fortress of Robert de Braybrooke, rebuilt in the reign of King John, and demolished in 1633.

The bridge of brown ironstone which spans this tributary of the River Welland was started by a descendant of the Crusader Sir Thomas whose effigy is in the church. It was completed on the instructions of his widow.

It has a low parapet, triple arches and two cutwaters.

ANCIENT BRIDGE

THIS TRIPLE ARCHED (TWO VISIBLE) STONE BRIDGE WITH TWO CUTWATERS, WAS STARTED BY SIR THOMAS LATIMER OF BRAYBROOKE CASTLE, WHO DIED IN 1401 AND COMPLETED IN ACCORDANCE WITH THE WILL OF HIS WIFE WHO DIED THE FOLLOWING YEAR. THE PARAPET IS RECENT

FINEDON – ROUND HOUSE

Location: On the A510 two miles north of the village. OS 141 934748

THIS eye-catching round house, known as Wellington Tower, was built by General Arbuthnot after the Duke of Wellington had been his guest at Woodford House. On that occasion the great commander had remarked on the similarity of the surrounding countryside to the terrain over which the Battle of Waterloo was fought.

To commemorate his visit his host built this circular tower of stone, topped by a chimney and balcony. A large plaque bears the words:

Panorama
Waterloo Victory
June 18 AD 1815

GEDDINGTON – DEER LEAP AT BOUGHTON HOUSE

Location: From the A43 at Geddington on back road from Geddington to Grafton Underwood. OS 141 908814

A DEER leap forms an integral part of the extensive boundary wall of the Boughton House estate.

Deer, which are still to be seen in the tranquil park, would be driven from the surrounding forest and leap over the wall on the inside of which the drop is considerable.

They were unable to leap out again, and thus swelled the numbers of the resident herd. It was one of the privileges accorded to the Lord of the Manor.

Boughton House – 'a vision of Louis XIV's Versailles transported to England' – is owned by the Duke of Buccleuch and Queensberry.

It stands in an estate of 11,000 acres which is administered by the Living Landscape Trust and here can be seen many aspects of the work of a great agricultural estate – farming, conservation, forestry and the rearing of game.

The park with its lakes, picnic and woodland play areas, shop and tearoom, is open from May to September. Boughton House, with its seventeenth and eighteenth century French and English furniture, tapestries and paintings by such artists as El Greco, Murillo and Caracci, and its Armoury, is open in the month of August only.

GRAFTON UNDERWOOD – MEMORIAL WINDOW

> *Location:* St James Church in Grafton Underwood, four miles east of Kettering.
> OS 141 922802

THIS stunning stained glass window showing a Flying Fortress coming home from a combat mission is one of two memorials here to the 384th Bombardment Group (Heavy) of the US Eighth Air Force.

It flew more than 9,000 sorties, and sadly lost 1,579 personnel, when it was based at Grafton Underwood in World War II.

The second, a granite memorial constructed 1971, is on the roadside perimeter of the airfield which covered 500 acres and from which the Flying Fortresses flew their first and last missions over Europe in 1943 and 1945 respectively.

HARRINGTON – VAMPING HORN

> *Location:* Church of St Peter and St Paul. Harington is three miles from Rothwell, right off the B576. OS 141 778805

ONE of the few surviving vamping horns in the country – there is another at Braybrooke – is protected by a glass case in the church on the outskirts of Harrington. It is five foot long and made of brass.

Vamping horns were used after the Restoration, possibly to summons people to church or to inspire the choir to greater efforts. In the open air they carry the human voice for up to a mile.

In the large churchyard are buried many of the men who fell on the field of battle at Naseby, six miles to the west, on 14 June 1645. Cavalier and Roundhead lie in the same ground, having fought to the death to decide who should rule them – the king or Parliament.

HARRINGTON – THE FALLS

NOT far from the Tollemache Arms, where a row of mature chestnut trees tower over a long stone wall, a fingerpost indicates the footpath leading to The Falls. Now only vague earthworks are all that remain of the manor house which stood above the cascading terraces.

One of its occupants of noble family, said to be Lady Jane Stanhope, is the central character in the legend of the White Lady.

She was pampered as a child, it is said, and was of a wilful disposition and insistent on getting her own way. Her faithful attendant was the old gardener, who was oblivious to her whims and tantrums.

When she grew up Lady Jane was often to be found tending to the widespread gardens with her aged retainer. One day, she saw him trample on one of the flowerbeds, albeit unwittingly, and flew into a temper. Taking up the nearest weapon – it happened to be a spade – she smashed him over the head with it and the old man expired.

Now filled with anguish for her horrible deed her wraith floats over The Falls at night, head bowed in remorse. A sighting of the White Lady is said to be a portent of a death.

ISHAM – SHEILA-NA-GIG AND PHEASANT ON THE THATCH

> *Location*: On the A509, three miles south of Kettering. OS 141 885739

FROM each corner of the square battlemented tower of St Peter's church, which is floodlit at night, strange gargoyles in stone look out over the village below.

Pne of them appears to be a female fertility symbol – perhaps the Sheila-na-gigs of Celtic legend – and they have been gazing down for many centuries.

Next to church, on the porch roof of a cottage appropriately called Little Thatches, is this cleverly crafted pheasant.

KETTERING – STATUE OF JERRY

Location: Wicksteed Park, on the A6 on the south eastern outskirts of the town.
OS 141 880773

WICKSTEED PARK was given to the people of Kettering for their leisure and recreation by Charles Wicksteed, who at the age of twenty one set up his own business in Kettering making steam ploughing machines. In 1876 he built his own factory and began producing marine tools After the First World War he turned to the manufacture of playground equipment.

His benevolence extended to the setting up of a charitable trust to support Wicksteed Park, which covers more than 150 acres and was opened in 1920.

In later life, he was frequently to be seen with his dog, Jerry, a Lakeland terrier to whom he was devoted, watching the progress of his developing parkland.

When his master was away on a business venture to South Africa, Jerry disappeared and was never seen again.

An Italian sculptor was commissioned to carve a stone statue of Jerry, and this touching memorial to a man's best friend can still be seen in the sunken garden beneath the bandstand. On a plaque on the plinth is written:

To the memory of Jerry 1920-28
The constant companion of Charles Wicksteed

Closely bound to a human heart
Little brown dog
You had your part
In the levelling,
Building, Staying of Streams,
In the Park That
Arose from Your
Master's Dreams.

KETTERING – STATUE OF JERRY

Jerry – the little brown dog who played his part.

ORLINGBURY – EFFIGY OF JOHN DE WITHMALE

Location: St Mary's church. Turn east off the A509 at Isham. OS 141 859724

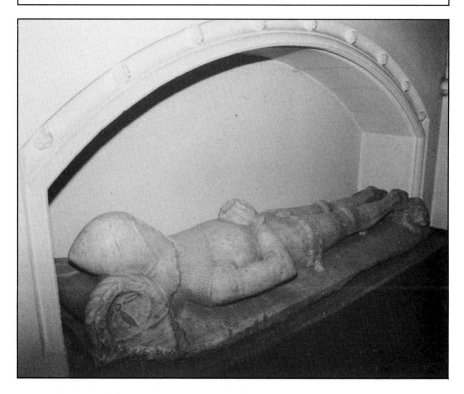

THIS is the effigy of the slayer of the last wild boar in England – or so it is said. A fourteenth century legend has it that John de Withmale, also known as Jack of Badsaddle (now a deserted village) came across the king and his entourage hunting in Rockingham Forest.

Suddenly, a wild boar charged at the king's horse and the royal rider was thrown to the ground. Jack raised his bow and fired an arrow that stopped the boar dead in its tracks before it could savage the fallen monarch with its tusks.

As a reward Jack was immediately dubbed Sir John de Withmale and received a grant of land. He died in 1375. Another version of this tale says that he shot the last wolf in the forest and died in doing so.

RINGSTEAD – STEPPING STONES

Location: Down a lane about one mile south of Ringstead, on the A 605 south east of Kettering. OS 141 968746

LYING somewhat overgrown and neglected in the river valley are these roughly squared stones which had a practical part to play in an area once liable to flood. They were on the footpath from the villages of Little and Great Addington up on the hill, to the railway station, now long since gone.

ROTHWELL – SKULLS IN THE CRYPT

Location: Holy Trinity church. Rothwell is on the A6 three miles north west of Kettering. OS 141 817811

BENEATH the south aisle of the nave of the longest parish church in the county lies a massive mound of skulls and thigh bones dating from the thirteenth century. They are the remains of some 1,500 bodies.

The grisly discovery of this crypt, or charnel house, was made in 1700, by a sexton in the course of grave digging. The remains were collected together in 1912 and today can be seen in the eerie surroundings in which they were found. The skulls and thigh bones – assumed to be those of medieval males, whose bones would have been more substantial and less likely to disintegrate then those of females – were assembled to await the Resurrection.

The crypt is open on Sundays from 2pm to 4pm from Easter to the end of September.

ROTHWELL – JESUS HOSPITAL

Location: Lower Market Place

IN 1591 Owen Ragsdale, a master at the Grammar School and a Fellow of Magdalene College, founded this almshouse for twenty-six elderly men and a house-keeper. The men wore blue coats and received a monetary allowance and other 'small mercies' from those less needy. Through the gate-way can be seen the cobbled courtyard and the date of 1593 above the archway.

Nearby, in the grounds of Rushton Hall, is the Triangular House built by Sir Thomas Tresham in 1593 to symbolise the Trinity. The building has three sides, three floors – in fact three of almost everything. It is now owned by English Heritage and open from April to September.

THRAPSTON – MILLSTONES

> *Location:* Denford Road, Thrapstone. On the A14 about eight miles west of Kettering. OS 141 993782

FROM the days of the Domesday survey, when 155 of them were recorded in the county, watermills have been used to grind grain into flour, wherever there was water power available.

There are now only two working watermills in the county, one at Bugbrooke and the other at Wellingborough, but many old millstones have survived and are used, as they are on either side of this gate, for decorative rather than practical purposes.

TWYWELL – LIVINGSTONE RELICS

Location: Church of St Nicholas at Twywell, off the A14 Kettering to Thrapston road. OS 141 952782

THE eleventh century church of St Nicholas has an unexpected connection with David Livingstone, and its other treasures include stones sent by General Gordon from Calvary in 1880.

The church's rector from 1874 to 1895 was the Reverend Horace Walker who, as a member of the Universities Mission in Africa, was instrumental in the freeing of slaves in Zanzibar. His close relationship with the famous explorer resulted in the publication of *The Last Journals of David Livingstone* after they were brought back to England by his servants, Susi and Chuma.

These two faithful followers had tended their master in his trials and cared for him in sickness. When he died in May 1873, they buried his heart and bound his body, to carry it 800 miles across hazardous country to the coast, and eventually to his homeland and burial at Westminster Abbey.

These brave men were taken in by the rector of Twywell and lived for the rest of their lives in the village.

COTTESBROOKE – VICTORIAN POSTBOX

Location: Off the A50 Northampton to Leicester road. OS 141 710735

COTTESBROOKE is a truly rural village with no shop, no pub and no Post Office. However, it does have a Victorian postbox, about which the residents feel most strongly.

There was a great outcry some years ago when the Post Office was closed and a new letter-box on a pole was provided and the original one removed.

In the end the protests were heeded and the box with its VR monogram returned to its place in the wall.

EAST HADDON – VILLAGE PUMP

Location: Off A428 Northampton to Rugby road.
OS 152 668682

IN the 1800s, when this village was a thriving farming community, there were more than a dozen pumps to draw water from the wells.

This pretty thatched pump still stands where two roads meet, and the circular water tower, built in 1890, is still behind the Post Office. At the start water was manually pumped up to the tank by the village blacksmith, then a less strenuous mechanical method was used until the mains supply was introduced in 1956 and the tower became redundant.

ECTON – SCRATCH OR MASS DIAL

Location: Church of St Mary Magdalene, Ecton, on the A4500 Northampton to Wellingborough.OS 152 829636

ON the doorway of the south porch of the Church of St Mary Magdalene is a worn scratch or mass dial. These ecclesiastical 'clocks', usually carved in the south wall of the church to be in full sunlight, acted as indicators for the time of Mass.

They were set at about head height and had lines from the central point scratched into the face of softer stone. As on a sundial, a gnomon or hand set in the hole, cast a shadow denoting the hour for worship.

Nearby is the Worlds End pub. Its inn sign depicts soldiers engaged at the Battle of Naseby, which was the end of the world for many thousands of men, both victorious Roundheads and defeated Cavaliers.

GRAND UNION CANAL – IRON TRUNK

Location: On the canal about one mile from the bridge at Cosgrove, for which turn east off the A508 Northampton to Milton Keynes road. OS 152 800412

FOLLOWING an Act of Parliament in 1793, the Grand Junction Canal Company began building a commercial waterway between Braunston in Northamptonshire through Buckinghamshire and Hertfordshire to the Thames at Brentford, engineers had many obstacles to overcome.

The canal was constructed in two parts, which met at Cosgrove, where it had to cross the Great Ouse into Buckinghamshire

Temporary locks, traces of which can still be seen, where built in 1800, and replaced five years later by an arched aqueduct. However, this collapsed and a temporary trough was installed until the present Iron Trunk aqueduct was made at Ketley Iron Works.

It was designed by William Jessop and is 101 feet long, fifteen feet wide and stands thirty six feet above the river.

There is access for pedestrians to the river bank and wildlife sanctuary at Ouse Valley Park through a tunnel or 'cattle creep' under the canal.

GRAND UNION CANAL – MILEPOST

> *Location*: On the towpath, south east of Cosgrove, near to lock. OS 152 795422

THE Grand Junction Canal Company's northern district engineer, Thomas Milner, set about measuring the entire length of the waterway with a steel tape and ordered cast iron mileposts to be made.

He was based at Gayton Junction and decided to reverse the earlier method of numbering and start from Braunston, a task he completed in 1893.

Many of these distinctive markers are now missing and the Northampton branch of the Inland Waterways Association, with the assistance of British Waterways, has undertaken a scheme of replacement.

GRAND UNION CANAL – BRIDGES

Location: Access is from the bridge over the canal on the Milton to Gayton road.
OS 152 718553

A turnover or roving bridge for horses to cross the canal without their towing ropes having to be unhitched.

Lift bridges were were installed along the canal so that farmers could get cattle across. The heavy top beams acted as a counterbalance so the bridge could be operated by one person.

HARLESTONE – A RACEHORSE REMEMBERED

Location: On the wall of Upper Harlestone sports field. Off the A428 Northampton to Rugby road. Cross the sports field behind the village hall and through two gaps in wall. The plaque is on the left. OS 152 698642

COTHERSTONE, a bay colt by Touchstone out of Emma, and owned by John Bowes of Streatham Castle, is commemorated by this plaque set into the wall of the sports field.

Although sickly as a yearling the horse, ridden by Bill Scott, won several races at Newmarket, including the 2,000 Guineas, and went on to win the 1843 Derby by two lengths.

Cotherstone won further races at Goodwood, but not the St Leger, and was ultimately sold to Lord Spencer.

KISLINGBURY – VILLAGE SIGN

THE village sign near to the church of St Luke shows an area steeped in history. Oliver Cromwell is said to have tethered his horse in this churchyard on the night before the Battle of Naseby.

The Parliamentarians, under the leadership of General Fairfax, were encamped in the surrounding fields, awaiting his arrival.

The Old Rectory, close by, is attributed to Francis Smith, the architect of Cottesbrooke Hall and the Rectory at Lamport.

49

LAMPORT – SWANS ON THE GATES OF LAMPORT HALL

Location: On the A508 to Market Harborough, eight miles from Northampton. OS 141 756745

THE Isham family crest, a white swan with raised wings, is depicted in cast iron on top of each of the square stone pillars at the drive entrance to Lamport Hall.

A branch of the family was established at Pytchley, near Kettering, where there was a swannery, as early as the fourteenth century.

John, the first of the Lamport Ishams, was a prosperous wool merchant. He purchased the manor in 1560 and eight years later built a new house, of which little now remains.

Architect Henry Hakewill, who designed the swan gates in 1824, was also engaged to undertake considerable alterations to the house by Mary Close, the Irish wife of Sir Justinian, the eighth baronet. It was she who planned the parkland, planting the fine cedars of Lebanon and sycamores that are still standing today.

Her son, Sir Charles Isham, who built Swan Lodge at the gates in 1850, was also a keen gardener. He created an unusual rock garden, which made a fitting setting for gnomes brought over from Nuremberg – the first of these little creatures to be featured in an English garden.

Sir Gyles Isham, the twelfth baronet, died unmarried in 1976 and the estate is now administered by the Lamport Hall Trust.

A local story concerning the swans relates that two young men, returning home somewhat the worse for wear, decided to paint the birds red. One of the swans, it is said, toppled from its pedestal, its beak piercing the chest of one of the miscreants, who paid with his life for this act of vandalism.

LITTLE BRINGTON– TILBURY BEACON

Location: On the old Roman road, Nobottle Belt, five and a half miles west of Northampton. OS 152 664633

THE anticipated invasion of England by the Spanish Armada in 1588 is recalled by this isolated beacon, erected to commemorate the 400th anniversary in July 1988.

It bears the coat of arms of the Spencers, on whose land it stands. The original beacon site was the thirteenth century tower of St Mary's Church at Great Brington.

There were also beacons on the towers of the churches at Ecton and Titchmarsh, and other sites were at Rockingham Castle, Ufford and Borough Hill.

Each position was chosen so that the smoke rather than the flames of the fire, could be seen from the greatest possible distance.

Nearby is Althorp House, the family home of Princes Diana and the Spencer family since 1508.

LITTLE HOUGHTON – ANIMAL HEADS

Location: On the wall of the butcher's shop near the crossroads. The village is off
the A428 Northampton to Bedford road. OS 152 802593

A TALENTED local worker in metal made the two animal heads which adorn the wall of the butcher's shop. One is a ram's head with curly horns and the other a bull with a ring through his nose.

Nearby, on the pavement outside the Post Office, are the village stocks. The last time they were put to use, it is said, was about a hundred years ago, when a local resident, William Baucutt, was confined by the ankles for drunkenness and ill-treating his spouse.

CLIFFORD HILL MOTTE

VISIBLE from north side of the road from Little Houghton to Cogenhoe, on the south bank of the River Nene, is a circular mound known as Clifford Hill.

It is more than fourteen metres high and surrounded by a deep ditch.

The top of the mound was levelled in Tudor times to make a bowling green, but this has long since disappeared.

MAIDWELL – VICTORIAN RAILWAY BRIDGE

Location: Not far from the car park at bottom of the hill between Maidwell and Draughton, off the A508. OS 141   755770

A BRANCH railway line from Northampton to Market Harborough was opened in 1859, although Castle Station at Northampton was not completed until 1885.

The line was closed in 1981 and purchased by Northamptonshire County Council six years later and transformed into the Brampton Valley Way, a linear country park of some fourteen miles in extent.

Labelled on existing plans as Bridge no. 18A, this fine example of a Victorian footbridge spans the Way where the public footpath links Maidwell and Draughton.

Nearby is All Saints church at Brixworth, the oldest church north of the Alps. It has Roman brick in it walls.

MOULTON – GATES AT HOLLY LODGE

Location: On the minor road to Boughton, north of Northampton. OS 152 770658

HOLLY LODGE was built in 1861 by Philadelphus Jeyes whose brother, John, formulated the well-known disinfectant, Jeyes Fluid.

The gates are patterned with a miscellany of Victorian farm implements including a fork, two pitchforks, a pair of sickles, a scythe, an axe, a hay rake, spade, hoe and flail.

Among other interesting features of Holly Lodge is the archway flanked by pillars with stone panels in which chubby cherubs are depicted.

NORTHAMPTON – BECKET'S WELL

Location: In Bedford road, opposite the park. OS 152 762602

BECKET'S WELL, named after Thomas a Becket, Archbishop of Canterbury, is said to be the one from which he took a drink after his escape from Northampton Castle. He had been imprisoned there in 1164 to await trial for his opposition to Henry II's attempts to restrict the power of the church and the ecclesiastical courts.

He escaped from imprisonment disguised as a humble priest and is supposed to have been given shelter by the nuns of Delapre Abbey, along the Nene Valley at Hardwater Mill, before going into exile in France.

He was later pardoned and returned to his archbishopric, but in 1170 he was murdered in his own cathedral by the four knights, one of them a Northamptonshire man. They were acting on the king's request, uttered in anger: 'Will no one rid me of this turbulent priest?'

NORTHAMPTON – MADONNA AND CHILD AND THE CRUCIFIXION

Location: St Matthews Church, Kettering Road, OS 152 768622

IN the north transept of the church is Henry Moore's *Madonna and Child*, a powerful sculpture hewn from Hornton stone. It was the gift of the first vicar of the parish, Canon Rowden Hussey, in 1944.

Later on his son, the Reverend J W A Hussey, commissioned *The Crucifixion* by Graham Sutherland, which is in the south transept.

This stark painting with its angular lines was unveiled in 1946 and was greeted with certain reservations by some viewers and with a shock reaction by others.

Today these two sensitive and contrasting works of art are admired for their skilful revocation of tranquillity and pain respectively.

ACROSS the road, on the corner of The Racecourse, is a tram shelter made by the firm of D Rowell of London in the 1920s. It has survived the disappearance of the trams that were Northampton's first form of public transport – and the trolley buses that succeeded them.

NORTHAMPTON – VENTILATION CHIMNEY

Location: Anglia Water, Bedford Road, OS 152 766599

THIS ventilation chimney by the reconstructed sewage works is of fluted sandstone. It was designed by Hyde-Piddock, engineer to the Northampton Improvement Commissioners who were responsible for scavenging, paving and lighting. It is the old engine house chimney and was in use when the Commissioners were in control of the sewage works.

NORTHAMPTON – ELEANOR CROSS

> *Location:* On the A508 London road at Hardingstone, Northampton.
> OS 152 755582

ELEANOR of Castile was married to Edward I for thirty six years and bore him fifteen children. When she died at Harby in Nottinghamshire in 1290 the king ordered thirteen crosses to be erected in memory of his beloved queen at the places where the funeral cortege rested on its 150 mile journey south to Westminster Abbey.

Besides the one at Geddington, considered to be the finest of the three surviving memorials, the only other one still standing is at Waltham Cross. The one at Charing Cross, the last overnight resting place of the funeral cortege, is a replica. Most of them went during the Civil War.

It is recorded that a mason, William of Ireland, received the sum of £3 6s 8d for each statue of the queen that he carved.

Delapre Abbey, at the bottom of the hill on the site of the Cluniac monastery founded in 1145, is where the coffin would have rested.

STOKE BRUERNE – STONE TABLET

Location: In St Mary's Church, Stoke Bruerne, off the A508 seven miles south of Northampton. OS 152 741499

THERE is a puzzling inscription on this stone tablet which forms a part of the wall of the extended enclosure on the west side of the churchyard. It appears to read:

A 1893 D

ParsoN GavE

WardeN DrovE

ClerK MadE

SquirE PaiD

God Save The Queen

To Our Own God

To what does it refer, one wonders?

SYWELL – RESERVOIR PUMP

Location: Visitor Centre, Sywell Country Park, Washbrook Lane. Turn north off the A4500 at Earls Barton crossroads for Sywell. OS 152 832650

THIS remaining pump, one of two, was installed about 1942 when Sywell reservoir provided water for the expanding towns of Rushden and Higham Ferrers.

The site was taken over by Northamptonshire County Council in 1983 and opened as a country park two years later. It covers 140 acres.

The W H Allen pump, driven by a 110 horse power motor, was capable of pumping 750,000 gallons of water in each twenty four hour period.

In 1956 a primary filter house was built to allow more water to flow into the filtration system. Its machinery had to be run for long periods and it created a great deal of noise.

SYWELL – SHEEP WASH

Location: At the gates of Sywell Country Park

THE sheep wash near the gates of Sywell Country Park was used regularly up to 1934 by farmers to wash their animals prior to shearing.

It was fed by the bywash from the reservoir and fell into disuse when new regulations required the use of chemicals in the dipping process, which could have caused pollution to the stream.

TOWCESTER – FIRE MARKS

Location: Park Street, off Watling Street, Towcester. OS 152 695485

MORE than seventy fire marks have been recorded in this county. They date from the days when insurance companies had their own fire brigades and their crews would only deal with blazes on properties bearing the company's fire mark as proof that a premium had been paid.

Most usually seen are the marks of the Sun, County and Phoenix insurance companies. Each mark was numbered, made of lead and bore some visual reference to the issuing company – the Sun, for instance, being a sun, that of the Phoenix, a phoenix. The one between the two first floor windows on this house can be seen in close up to be that of a company which was based in Birmingham.

ALDWINCLE – RAISED WALKWAY

Location: On the minor road between Aldwincle and Thorpe Waterville, off the A605 from Thrapston. OS 141 016815

THIS stretch of slightly elevated pathway is now just a convenient leftover from the days when floods were common along this valley and not controlled as they are today.

Cars and their occupants were frequently stranded when the River Nene overflowed its banks between here and Brancey Bridge.

Today the panoramic view over the vast acres of the Titchmarsh Nature Reserve can be greatly enhanced from this handy grandstand.

ASHTON – DRAGONFLY MUSEUM

Location: Turn off the A605 Oundle bypass at the roundabout. OS 142 056883

ASHTON MILL, on the River Nene, in the most typical of English settings, is Europe's only museum devoted to the dragonfly.

The life-cycle of these endangered insects is clearly illustrated and the dragonfly sanctuary is a delight to the nature-lover, who might quickly convert to a dragonfly enthusiast.

The museum, gift shop and tea rooms are open at weekends from June to the end of September.

The National Dragonfly Museum
Ashton Mill

EASTON-ON-THE-HILL – PRIEST'S HOUSE

Location: In West Street, Easton-on-the-Hill. Off the A43 two miles south west of Stamford. OS 141 009046

THIS pre-Reformation priest's house, now administered by the National Trust, houses on the upper floor a small museum of bygones. The two storeys are connected by a stone newel stairway leading to the open timbered roof.

Nearby is Glebe House, once occupied by the rector's son, Captain Lancelott Skynner, master of the vessel *La Lutine* which sank off the coast of Holland in 1799 with a cargo of gold valued at £1,400,000. The Lutine Bell, from his ship, is rung by Lloyds of London – one stroke signifying bad news, two strokes heralding good news.

FOTHERINGHAY– REMAINS OF CASTLE

Location: Off the A605 three and a half miles south east of Oundle.
OS 142 061931

A GRIM collection of stones beside the River Nene is all that remains of Fotheringhay Castle where Mary, Queen of Scots was beheaded in February 1587. Her body reposed there in a lead coffin for some months before being taken to Peterborough cathedral. From there it was removed by her son James I, in October 1612, to rest in Westminster Abbey. Scottish thistles, affectionately called Queen Mary's Tears, still grow on the slopes of the mound.

In the main street and now a private house, stood the *New Inn* where Bull, the queen's executioner, was billeted.

NASSINGTON – STEPPING STONES

Location: About half a mile out of Nassington, on the Fotheringhay to Wansford road. OS 142 075966

STEPPING stones of an unusual design confront the walker along this section of the Nene Way.

The steps, on a secluded bend, are flat elevated squares of stone securely fixed on pegs. They span the tributary which forms the county boundary, where the Way briefly deviates into Cambridgeshire before crossing back over the River Nene at Yarwell Mill.

THORPE ACHURCH – MEMORIAL WELL

Location: Turn west off the A605 Thrapston to Oundle road on to the B662 and left at Lilford Hall gates. OS 141 023830

AN elaborately carved oak canopy with two guardian angels mounted on its supporting pillars, covers the well which bears a memorial inscription to Thomas Alberion Powys, formerly of nearby Lilford Hall. The trough from which the horses drank is still there as well as remains of the winding gear.

THORPE WATERVILLE – BARN GABLE END

Location: Off the A605 Thrapston to Oundle road, turn at the Fox Inn
OS 141 022816

SEEN from the road from Thorpe Achurch, the two circular windows and prominent chimney-breast on the end wall of this barn resemble a pair of soulful eyes staring from a mournful face.

The barn stands on the site of a fortified manor house, believed to have been destroyed in the Wars of the Roses.

Nearby, at Aldwincle, is Dryden House, where poet and playwright John Dryden was born in 1631.

WADENHOE – POSTAL TELEGRAPH OFFICE

Location: Off the A605 from Thrapston turning west at Thorpe Waterville
OS 141 012835

THE Postal Telegraph Office at Wadenhoe retains the name it was originally given and it has not called itself a post office. For here, indeed,was history in the making.

In his capacity as Chancellor of the Exchequer in Disraeli's Cabinet of 1868 The Right Honourable George Ward-Hunt, of the Wadenhoe Estate, was responsible for adding one penny to the rate of income tax to finance the Abyssinian War.

In consequence of his high office (he was also First Lord of the Admiralty), the first Postal Telegraph Office in England was set up here to keep him in touch with Government affairs.

Wadenhoe was also, in 1869, the first village to have its own gasworks

WOODNEWTON – COCO THE CLOWN'S GRAVE

Location: St Mary's Church, On minor road west of Fotheringhay. OS 141 033946

THIS neat village once stood in the midst of the Forest of King's Cliffe. A headstone in the peaceful graveyard of St Mary's marks the final resting place of the world famous character, Coco the Clown, who died in 1974.

Nicholai Polakovs, who was born in Russia, lived here in a caravan with his wife, Valentina, between his extensive travels abroad with the circus. Other members of his family also lived here and whenever he could he returned to this little community where he had made his home.

HIGHAM FERRERS – MARKET CROSS AND BEDE HOUSE

Location: In the centre of the town, which is east of Wellingborough at the junction of the A45 and A6. OS 153 962685

HIGHAM FERRERS is a small town with an impressive history. It became a borough in 1251, and in 1556 was granted the right to be represented in Parliament – a right it exercised until the Reform Act of 1832.

The present Town Hall overlooks the ancient Market Cross,which is surrounded by lovely old limestone houses.

Archbishop Chichelle,the son of a local draper, founded the Bede House, pictured right, in 1428 on the site of an earlier hospital.

It had living quarters for twelve poor men and a housekeeper, and had a raised chapel for worship at one end.

The Archbishop's School, which is opposite Bede House, was re-established by this great benefactor in 1422.

It was set up for educational purposes in 1391 and became a grammar school for almost three centuries.

HIGHAM FERRERS – BEDE HOUSE

EARLS BARTON – HOBBING FOOT

Location: Museum in Barkers Factory Yard, Earls Barton is on the A4500
Northampton to Wellingborough road. OS 152 852638

THE Earls Barton Museum houses many objects associated with the footwear trade. Among them is this 'hobbing foot' or 'clencher', a shoemaker's tool incorporating four different sizes. A three feet model is more usual.

The museum is open on Saturdays only, from 10am to 4pm

THIS cast iron lion's head was at one time, prior to the alignment of the road in 1970, in the wall of the old vicarage garden and spring water gushed from its mouth into a horse trough.

The trough has long gone but the tablet from it, inviting the traveller to 'drink freely from the water of life' has been placed beside the lion's head in its new location.

IRCHESTER –BREAD OVEN AND SHELF

Location: In St Katherine's Church. Three miles south of Wellingborough, on the B570, east of the A509. OS 152 826660

THIS Jacobean bread shelf is mounted high on the wall of the north aisle and there is a rare thirteenth century bread oven and chimney shaft in the north wall of the chancel. It was used not only to bake bread for the altar, but for the poor of the parish.

The church is dedicated to Katharine of Alexandra who is thought to have been tortured on the wheel that takes her name and then beheaded in 307AD for professing her Christianity. A stained glass window of 1926 depicts scenes from her life.

The weathervane on the 160ft spire is in the form of a Catherine wheel, within a shield

IRCHESTER – STEAM LOCOMOTIVE

Location: Narrow Gauge Railway Museum, Irchester Country Park. The entrance is on the B570. OS 152 910660

ONE of the engines in a musuem devoted to the restoration, display and demonstration of industrial narrow gauge locomotives and their accessories is this magnificent steam locomotive – a Peckett 0-6-0, tank 1870/1934, works number 85. It was once in constant use hauling ironstone from the

pits at Sidegate Lane and Finedon Road, to the ironworks at Wellingborough.

The strange instrument, right, is the precursor to the crowbar – the Jim Crow. It was used on industrial railways, where frequent changes in track layout were required, to bend rails *in situ*, either cold or with the application of heat. It was easily portable and could be operated by two or three men.

The museum is open on Sundays and Bank holidays.

RUSHDEN – Strainer arch

Location: St Marys church, Rushden. OS 153 958666

THE secret of the strength of St Mary's church lies in the famous strainer arch, of about 1370, of which there are only a few examples in this country.

The ornately decorated arch which spans the nave, was inserted to support the tall north/south walls and prevent them from leaning inward.

The arch is of handsome tracery, which had become choked with whitewash over the years until a nineteenth century curate, the Reverend F M MacCarthy, diligently removed it to reveal the lace-like stonework in its true glory.

SET for all eternity in alabaster, kneeling at a prayer desk opposite his second wife Mary, with their eight children at prayer below, is Sir Robert Pemberton, a gentleman usher at the court of Queen Elizabeth I.

Their marriage was a happy one, according to the rhyme on the monument:

> By God's grace we so evenly were paired
> As that in sexes equally we shared;
> We had eight children to augment our joys,
> For her four daughters and for me four boys.

WELLINGBOROUGH – GREAT FIRE PLAQUE

Location: Set on an inside wall of 23 Silver Street, Wellingborough
OS 152 891678

HANNAH BURKE must have been a resourceful woman for she saved her house in Pebble Lane from destruction by fire by dousing it with ale. However, more than 200 houses, 800 shops and other buildings were lost in the busy, crowded town on the afternoon of Friday, 28 July 1738 in the Great Fire of Wellingborough.

It is thought to have been started by a lad drying oats in the area of Silver Street and the plaque marks the spot where flames, fanned by the wind, could no longer be controlled by the primitive fire fighting methods of those days. The fire was ultimately halted by cutting a fire-break along Canon Street, as had been done in the Great Fire of London.

Damage to property amounted to £16,090 3s and loss of personal belongings to £9,896 2s 10d. Surrounding towns made generous contributions in guineas, goods and elbow grease to assist with the rebuilding.

INDEX TO PLACES